DREAMSCAPES

Pour Anne,

Avec plaisir,

André Gallant ☺

DREAMSCAPES

Exploring Photo Montages

ANDRÉ GALLANT

AN ANDRÉ GALLANT BOOK

For your love, support and the good values you've instilled in me,
this book is dedicated to you, Mom, with love.

National Library of Canada Cataloguing in Publication

Gallant, André
Dreamscapes : exploring photo montages / André Gallant.

ISBN 0-9734714-0-9

1. Photomontage.   2. Photography--Technique.   I. Title.

TR685.G34 2004   778.8   C2004-900135-3

CONTENTS

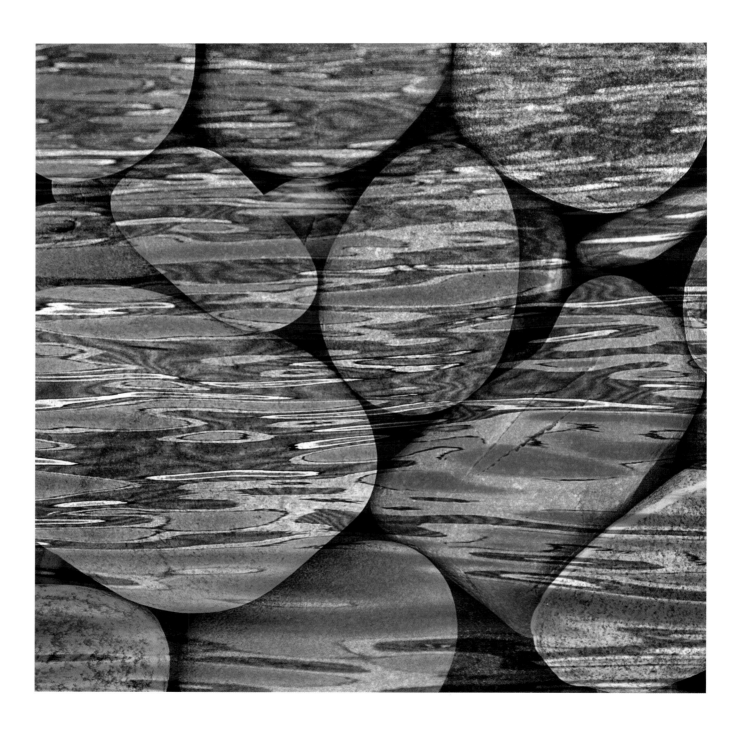

PREFACE

In my early twenties, I became passionate about photography. I bought all the books I could find on the subject, devoured the text and admired the photographs. I remember reading about slide sandwiches the combination of two unrelated images. (Photo montages is a more appropriate term.) The examples used to illustrate the text had very little effect on me. I didn't give it much thought, as I was too new at photography to fully appreciate the technique. I had yet to learn the basic skills needed to make a good photograph.

A few years ago, while I was editing a couple of rolls of film, I accidentally dropped two slides, one on top of the other. I was fascinated by the mystical appearance of the superimposed images. It reminded me of the montage technique I'd come across so long ago. I began combining slides and was very excited with some of the results. I was also experimenting with double exposures, with the first in focus and the second out of focus, and wondered whether I could achieve the same effect using two pieces of film. At first my exposures were way off, and the results were too dark. As I did more montages, the results improved. I sought magazine and book articles on the subject, and after further experimentation, "dreamscapes" were born, fulfilling my need for deeper expression through photography.

I've embraced this technique and have rediscovered the magic of making photographs. The overwhelming response to these images is what inspired me to write and illustrate this book. I continue to explore, and look forward to the discoveries that lie ahead. *Dreamscapes* is about evocative imagery derived from one's fantasy.

ANDRÉ GALLANT
DECEMBER 2003

INTRODUCTION

Experimenting with montages a few years ago, I rediscovered the joy of photography. Although I still loved working with a camera, making photographs on a daily basis had lost some of its appeal. Since the evening I dropped two slides one on top of the other and became aware of a new world emerging from those two tiny pieces of film, I've been hooked on montages, and I'm constantly excited as I explore and discover.

Because of their appearance, I refer to all photo montages as "dreamscapes." In this book I will explain the four different types of dreamscapes I create, and teach you how to make your own. I've given each type a descriptive name to distinguish between them and avoid confusion. *Composite dreamscapes* are made by combining two unrelated images. *Mirror dreamscapes* are made by inverting a single image vertically, horizontally, or both, and superimposing it on the original image. *Surreal dreamscapes* are made by combining an in-focus image with an out-of-focus image of the same scene. *Cross dreamscapes* combine a vertical image with a horizontal one to produce a square image. Other terms for these montages may exist.

All the dreamscapes in this book were made using slides. It is possible to create montages with negatives, but unless you print your own photographs it will become a task for the photo labs to produce these for you. I'm often asked why I don't produce my dreamscapes digitally. I love transparency film and know it well, and I need slides for teaching. I also love the instantaneous results. I photograph specifically for montages, and by making my dreamscapes manually I get a better sense of what works. I still get excited when I open a box of newly developed slides and view the results of a good shoot. I spend a lot of time (especially on inclement days) at my light table creating interesting combinations of various images. I'm often surprised by what looks good together. The subjects you combine are entirely up to you, and will reflect your personality.

When you combine slides, you need to use images that are light in tone to obtain a properly exposed montage. Alternatively, you can overexpose the photographs you intend to pair for your dreamscapes. When you are ready to put a montage together, I recommend using GEPE glassless slide mounts. When handling film, use cotton gloves at first so you don't leave fingerprints on the film. Peel both slides from their mounts, align them and insert the film under the two small tabs found on the dark grey part of the mount (I loosen them by inserting a fingernail under each). If I'm going to project my dreamscapes, I get a professional lab to make duplicates. Moisture often gets between the layers of film, and the heat from a projector lamp will cause them to stick together, leaving noticeable marks.

The digital darkroom is a wonderful tool to help you fine-tune your dreamscapes. With Photoshop you can lighten or darken your images as needed. Using layers, you can create mirror and cross montages with a single image, whether slide, print or digital photo. Simply duplicate your image, rotate and/or reverse it and blend the result with the original image into a dreamscape. Or, again using layers, you can combine two different images to produce surreal and composite montages. By combining images digitally you avoid the problem of Newton rings (circular patterns that sometimes occur when two pieces of film are held closely together), which often plague montages made with slides.

In the chapters that follow, I'll explain how to create each type of dreamscape in more detail. I'll show you some sample montages, and fill you in on how I achieved the results. These examples will help you begin your own explorations. Finally, for each technique I include two photo essays that demonstrate the passion and power evoked by dreamscapes.

Calla lily with rusted metal surface

COMPOSITE DREAMSCAPES

The "composite dreamscape" is a photo montage made by combining two unrelated images. When using slide film, you can combine bright scenes (tonally light subject matter). You'll have to overexpose your photographs when dark tones and colours prevail. Although Photoshop is very useful for lightening your photographs, I do most of my montages manually. So if I photograph an image with dark subject matter (forest, dense foliage, etc.) for a montage, I usually add a stop or two of light (+1, +2).

Your first attempt at creating composite dreamscapes may yield better results if part of your montage is a texture (peeling paint, water ripples, fabric, pebbles). Combining that texture with a scene (a meadow, an orchard, flowers) will add a painterly quality to your dreamscape. Most of my favourites have been achieved this way, so I am always on the lookout for interesting textures. I take a series of photographs, bracketing as I overexpose (+1, +2, +3). Having a choice of photographs with different degrees of lightness improves the success rate of my composite dreamscapes.

Many of my montages have been created with images taken years apart. I now keep most of my overexposed images — mistakes and planned — in my files for later use. None of them ever goes to waste.

On the next pages are examples of composite dreamscapes that appeal to me. You may choose to combine completely different images. The beauty of photography is that each photographer develops a unique style.

On the opposite page is the result of a combinaton of the two images above. Neither slide needed to be overexposed. Photographed in Namibia, the silhouetted trees at sunrise stand out dramatically against the tonally light image of a sand dune. The contrast adds starkness to the dreamscape. It is a good marriage of these two scenes.

I was looking for some new composite dreamscapes for this book and decided to have a look in my "winter" files. I pulled out about twenty different slides and started combining them, hoping to find an interesting dreamscape. The combination (shown above) of the fence with warm light on the snow and the snowdrifts with cool hues struck me as beautiful and surreal.

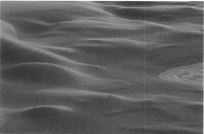

I have a few boxes of slides marked "montaging material." I opened one up and grabbed two slides, and this scene appeared before my eyes. Serendipity? A photograph of branches covered with ice (photographed in 1993 in Manitoba for the book *Winter*, which I illustrated for Pierre Berton) is combined with a photograph of two church windows with dew on the panes of glass. The overall yellow hue comes from out-of-focus autumn leaves outside the church windows.

 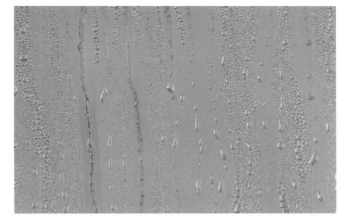

The image on the opposite page is a combination of the photographs above, a white calla lily and dew on a window pane reflecting orange autumn hues. Because both images were tonally bright, I obtained a properly exposed dreamscape without overexposure. The texture of the dew drops softens the flower, and the colour is harmonious.

Photographed ten years ago for the book *Winter*, the slides above were simply filed away. The montage on the right has brought life back into these old images, one of the pleasures of creating dreamscapes.

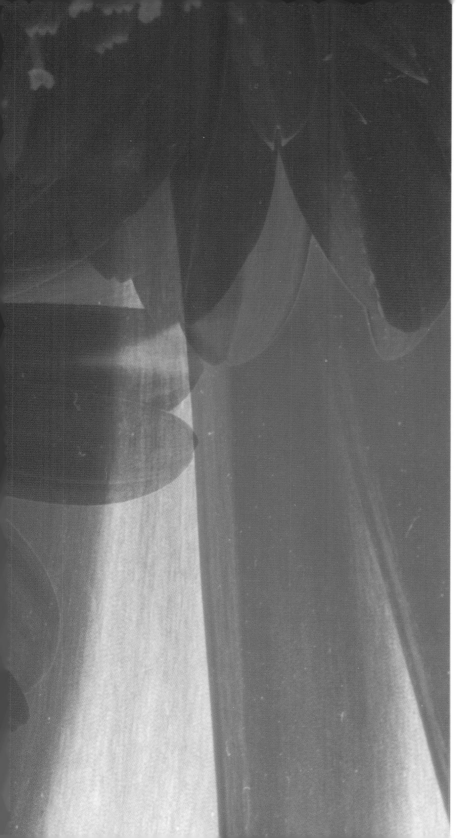

A BOUQUET FOR MY MOTHER

*"A mother understands
what a child does not say."*

JEWISH PROVERB

Above: anthurium flower with tombstone texture

Opposite: two shots of a gerbera daisy

Above: impatiens flowers with rough painted wall

Opposite: gaura with cracked white paint

Tulip and textured glass

Parrot tulip and multiple exposure of grass

Above and opposite: tulips and thick, coloured glass

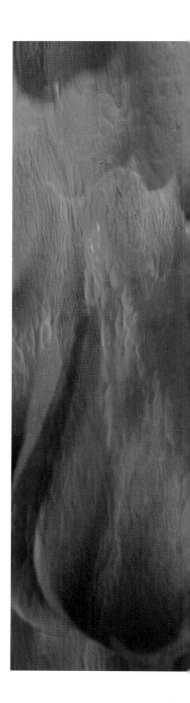

Above and opposite: poppy petals and water drops on plastic

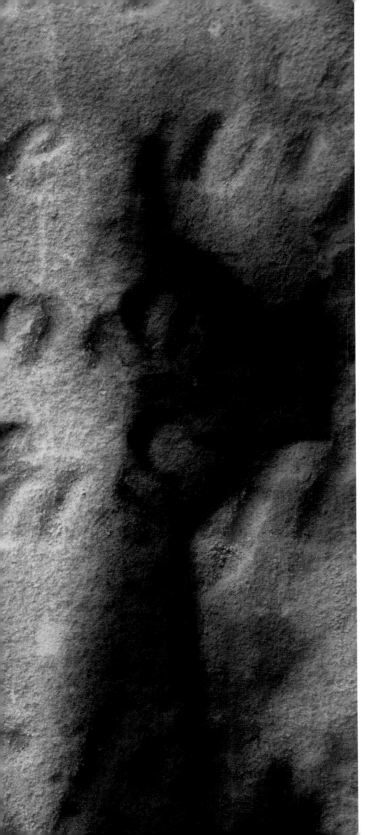

REQUIEM

"I'll meet you on the other side."

<small>DAVID GRAY</small>

Above: gravestone and detail of pansy

Opposite: gravestone and stone cross

Gravestone and wet rocks

Gravestone and hydrangea blooms

Above: gravestone and out-of-focus leaves against blue sky

Opposite: gravestone and multiple exposure of tree

Gravestone and tulips

Gravestone and dahlia

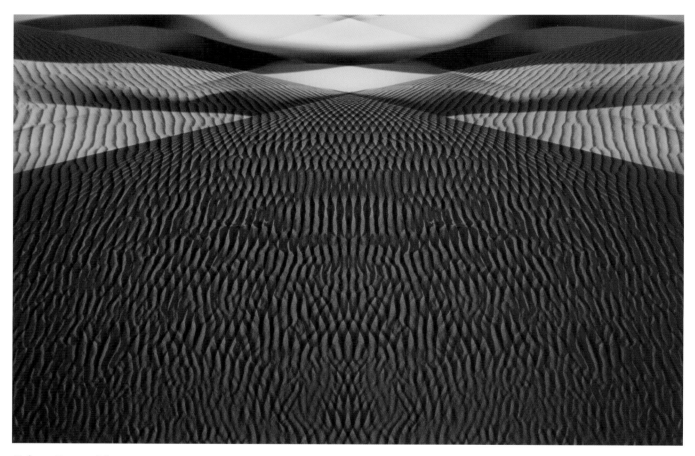

Sahara Desert, Morocco

MIRROR DREAMSCAPES

To create "mirror dreamscapes," you will need two identical slides of an image — or, if you work with Photoshop, you can use one image and create a duplicate. There are three different ways you can combine the identical images:

1) By inverting one of the slides or images (turning it upside down, or rotating it 180 degrees) then positioning it on top of the other.
2) By reversing one of the slides or images (turning it over from left to right, or flipping it horizontally) then positioning it on top of the other.
3) By inverting and rotating one of the slides or images (turning it over from top to bottom, or flipping it vertically) then positioning it on top of the other.

Each combination will produce an intriguing mirror-like result. Play with the different ways of pairing them and choose the version that works best. It may seem as if you're viewing the images through a kaleidoscope.

Images with lines and shapes that crisscross when inverted or reversed are most effective for this type of dreamscape. The process becomes pure abstracting, and the results can be very powerful because of the perfect symmetry. If you're producing these montages manually, you'll need to overexpose when shooting the images. In the following examples, I've recorded the settings I used to give you an idea of how much exposure is required.

The symmetry in mirror dreamscapes adds impact. To create the dreamscape of the stained glass window above, I reversed one of the slides (flipping it horizontally, from left to right) and then combined the two. Because the image is light in tone, it did not need to be overexposed. The montage becomes mysterious because of the converging glass panes in the middle of the image.

1. original photo

2. reversed photo

To create the mirror dreamscape above, I used two identical slides, reversing one (flipping the slide horizontally, left to right) over the other. The original photographs were overexposed by one stop each. The heavy overcast sky added a coolness to the hues. It is interesting to see that the leaves that merge with the pavement become textured, while those that overlap stand out against the background.

With two identical slides of an agave plant, the dreamscape above was created by reversing one of the images (flipping one slide horizontally) over the other. The slides were overexposed by one stop.

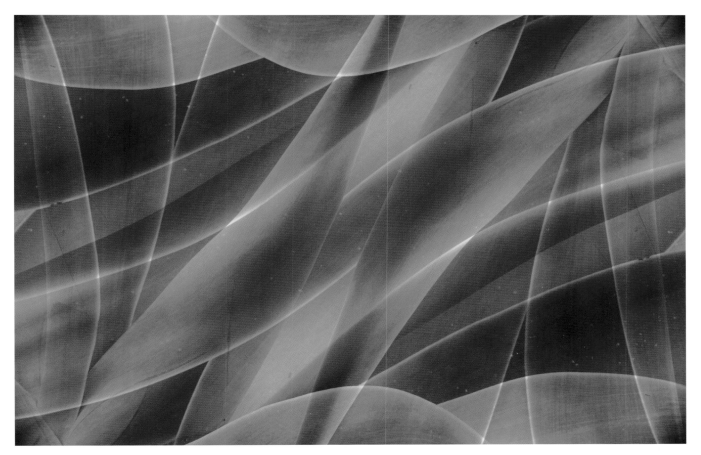

Using the same slides from the dreamscape on the opposite page, I inverted one of the images (rotated one slide 180 degrees) and positioned it on top of the other. Once combined, they produced the dreamscape above.

These trees, photographed in spring and autumn, demonstrate some of the possibilities when creating mirror montages. Both dreamscapes were made by reversing one image (flipping one slide horizontally) over the other. In both cases, the original slides were overexposed by one stop each.

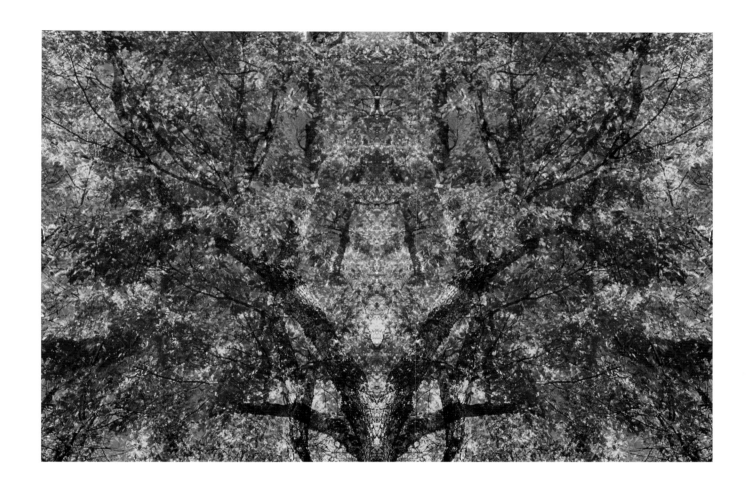

On a misty morning at Le Jardin Botanique du Nouveau Brunswick, I took two identical slides of a damselfly on wet grass (overexposing each by one stop). I was aware that when I turned these slides into a mirror montage, reversing one image over the other and combining the two, the damselfly's body would appear to merge into itself, thus creating an intriguing dreamscape.

I came upon this vine against a screen in New Zealand while teaching a workshop. I trusted my instincts and took two identical photographs, overexposing each by one and a half stops. This reversal mirror montage (I flipped one slide horizontally) is one of my favourites.

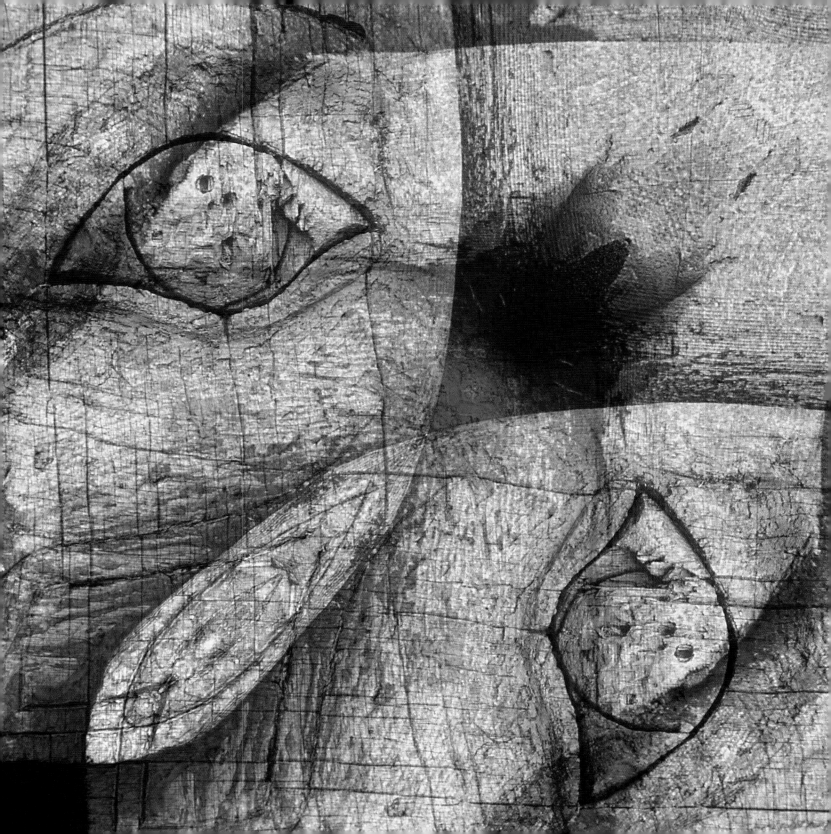

SPIRIT OF THE TOTEMS

"The task of my generation is to remember all what was taught."

SUSAN POINT, COAST SALISH ARTIST

Above and opposite: Prince Rupert, British Columbia

Right and opposite:
Thunderbird Park,
Victoria,
British Columbia

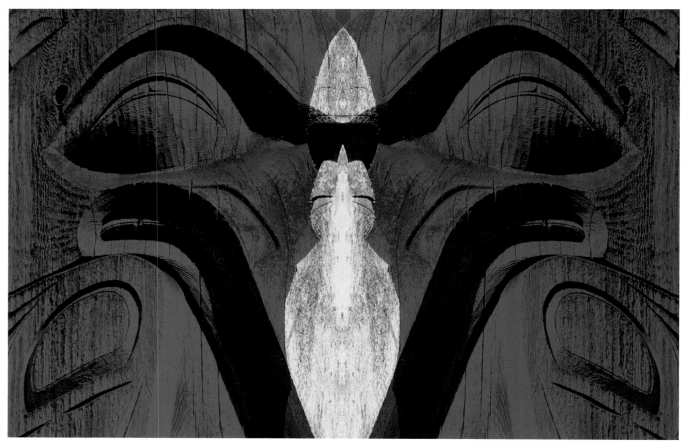

Above and opposite: Museum of Anthropology, Vancouver, British Columbia

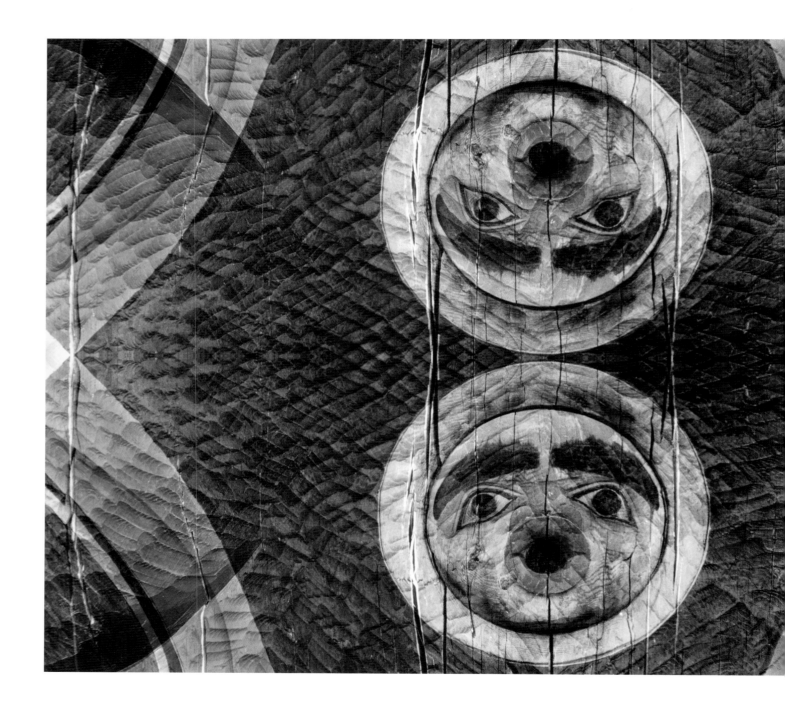

Above and opposite: Petersburg, Alaska

Right and opposite:
Museum of
Anthropology,
Vancouver,
British Columbia

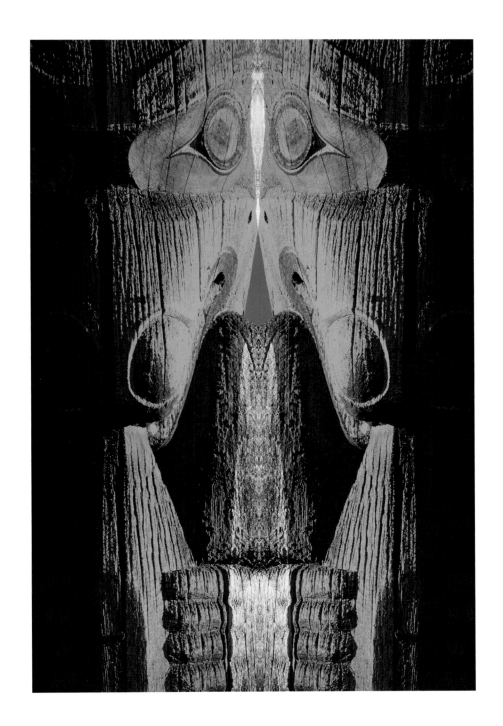

SEAS OF SAND

"Take only memories, leave nothing but footprints."

CHRIS SEATTLE

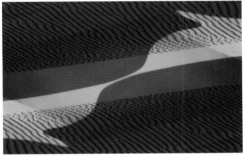

Above and opposite: Namib desert, Namibia

Above and opposite: Sahara desert, Morocco

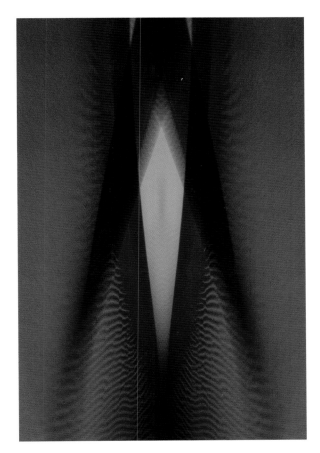

Above and opposite: Sahara desert, Morocco

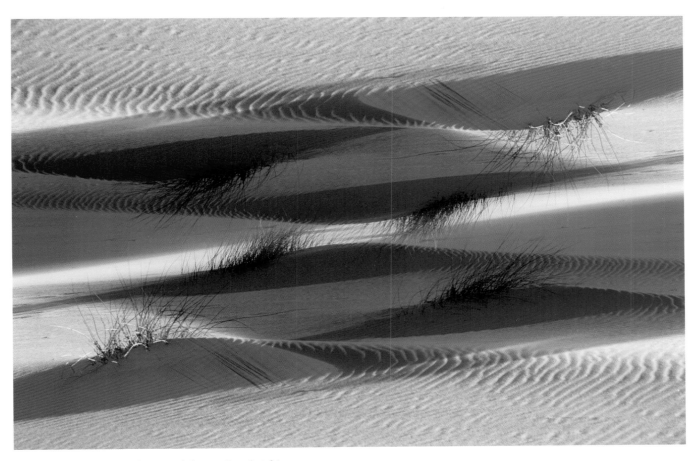

Above and opposite: White sand desert, South Africa

Willow City Loop, Texas

SURREAL DREAMSCAPES

"Surreal dreamscapes" are made by combining an in-focus image with an out-of-focus image of the same scene. This is the type of dreamscape preferred by most people. The glowing, saturated colours give the montages their surreal appearance. Dreamy, moody, romantic and timeless are a few words that can be used to describe them.

To achieve a successful montage, you will need a camera fitted with a lens, preferably a telephoto or zoom, in the range of 200mm to 300mm. A macro lens is also adequate. You may encounter difficulties using short lenses (wide angle and normal), as it is not always possible to obtain a defocused image without detail. Obviously, a tripod is necessary. Slow-speed slide films with saturated colours lend themselves well to surreal dreamscapes (Fuji Velvia 50 or 100, Kodak E100VS, G or GX).

With your camera on a tripod, shoot two versions of the same scene. The first photograph should be in focus and overexposed by two stops. The second shot should be thrown out of focus, with your lens set to its largest aperture (wide open, usually between f2.8 and f5.6). Overexpose the second shot by one stop. As you blur your second photo, make sure the scene enlarges as you are defocusing. Eliminate the details, but make sure you retain the shapes of the subject matter. The combination of the two slides should render a properly exposed dreamscape.

If you feel your results are too dark, you may want to add half a stop of brightness by overexposing the first (sharp) photograph by two and a half stops. On the other hand, if the outcome is too light, you will need to reduce the amount of overexposure. If you are new to the technique, experiment by taking extra slides, bracketing your exposures and varying the degree of defocus on the second image. When you get your film back and view the results, you'll be able to assess what's working well.

Surreal dreamscapes can also be made using three pieces of film, where one image is sharp and two are defocused. You will encounter a loss of detail, especially in the highlights, but the results will appear even more dramatic and surreal. When attempting this technique, overexpose the sharp slide by three stops, and overexpose both defocused shots, the first by one and a half stops, the second by two stops.

The best light for shooting surreal dreamscapes occurs in the early morning and early evening because of the quality and colour of light at these times. Warm, soft light enhances the technique, producing dramatic results. The use of backlight can also be extremely effective. On bright cloudy days, the colours will appear rich and saturated. Avoid shooting at midday when it's sunny and the light is strong and uneven—the parts of the image that fall into shaded areas will become too dark and will lose all detail.

Natural scenes lend themselves very well to this technique. I've had good success with montages of trees, meadows and flowers. I also enjoy doing surreal dreamscapes of abandoned houses, winding roads in the country and graveyards with old, weathered tombstones. Another favourite subject matter is old, corroding cars—especially the classics of the fifties. I love the way the metallic paint glows against the rust; the way the chromed bumpers, door handles and manufacturers' decals take on a ghostly appearance; the way the harshness of metals and broken glass is softened.

The surreal dreamscape on the opposite page is the result of combining the two images above. I took the photographs with my camera secured on a tripod. I backed away as far as I could from the chair and skates so I could use the highest magnification from my 70mm–300mm zoom lens. Overexposing the first frame by two stops, I took the photo at f16 to ensure good focus and sharpness. For the second frame, I threw the image out of focus, used my widest opening of f5.6 and overexposed by one stop.

When defocusing, I generally eliminate the details, but retain the shapes in the original scene. I then open up the lens to its widest aperture, usually between f2.8 and f5.6, depending on the lens used. (If I didn't use my widest aperture, the depth of field would increase and the out-of-focus part of my montage might not be defocused enough.) I then take my second photograph, overexposing by one stop. When I get my slides back, they look like the images above: the sharp one has all the detail, while the out-of-focus photo has most of the colour.

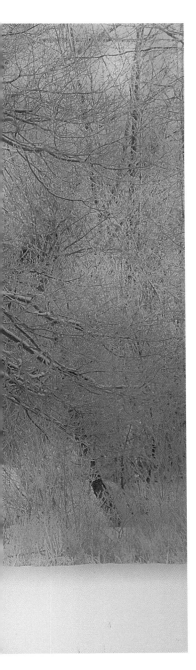

The surreal dreamscape of the tree was photographed using my 70mm–300mm lens. I backed away from the scene, which enabled me to photograph with the lens zoomed all the way to 300mm, making it easier to eliminate details when I need to defocus. The leaf in hoarfrost (below) was photographed using the same lens on its macro setting.

While shooting in Paris, I used the surreal dreamscape technique to add a dreamy quality and romantic mood to images of ancient masonry on Notre Dame cathedral (opposite) and the glorious Jardin de Luxembourg (above). With both of these images I used my 70mm–300mm zoom lens at the 300mm setting, which allowed me to effectively defocus the second part of my montage.

When I entered this graveyard in a small Mexican town, I was captivated by its colours. Noticing the skull in one of the bone repositories, I felt uneasy, as if someone was watching me. I knew that a surreal dreamscape of this scene would convey my feelings more accurately than regular photographs.

I like consistency in my work, and chose to shoot all of
my photographs of the graveyard as surreal dreamscapes.
The technique softens the colours and contrast of the
images. Surreal dreamscapes are most effective when
light subject matter appears against a dark background.
The halo created by the out-of-focus layer of the
dreamscape makes the gladioli stand out against the
darker hue of the blue tombstone.

The surreal dreamscape effect is not as noticeable in this image of a bilberry tree with spring blooms because the lighter part of the scene is not against a dark background. Nevertheless, there is a beautiful softness throughout.

The spider's web appears to glow, and stands out strongly against the darker hues in the background. For both this image and that of the bilberry tree, I followed the same exposure recipe: sharp image, plus two stops; blurred image, plus one stop.

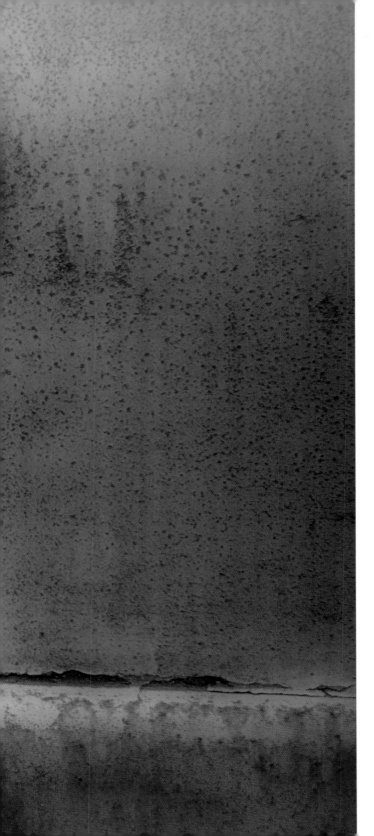

CORROSION

*"Art is not what you see,
but what you make others see."*

Edgar Degas

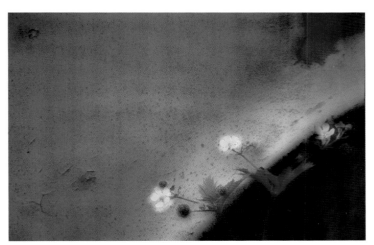

Above: Detail of an old truck wheel moulding, Alaska
Opposite: Detail of an old truck door and handle, Alaska

Above and opposite: fender and headlight of an old, rusty car, South Africa

Above: Odometer with lichen, New Zealand
Opposite: Broken headlight, New Zealand

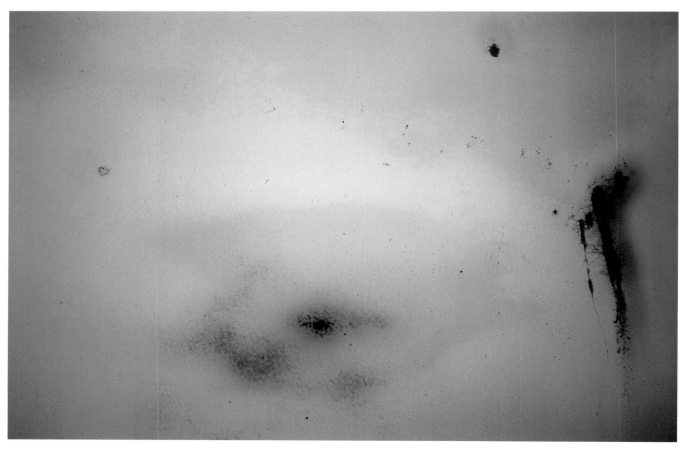

Above and opposite: Rusty details on door of a wrecked car, Kingston, New Brunswick

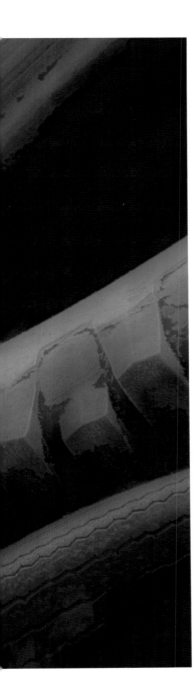

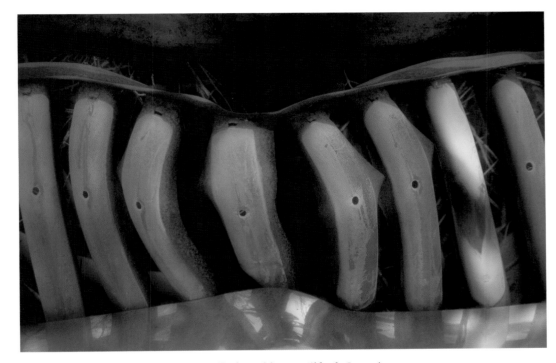

Above: Frost on bumper and front grill of an old car, Milford, Ontario
Opposite: Frost on tires, Milford, Ontario

Flowers coming out of the trunk of an old car, Milford, Ontario

Branch with grapes on car hood, Milford, Ontario

Above and opposite: Front of an old car, Milford, Ontario

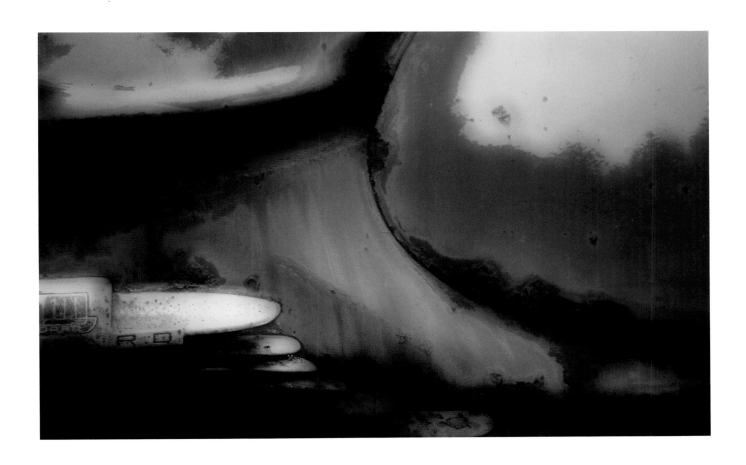

LYRICISM

"The stillness shall be dancing"

ADAPTED FROM "EAST COKER, FOUR QUARTETS"
BY T.S. ELIOT

Above and opposite: Tuscany, Italy

Above and opposite: Golan Heights, Israel

Above and opposite: Van Dusen Garden, Vancouver

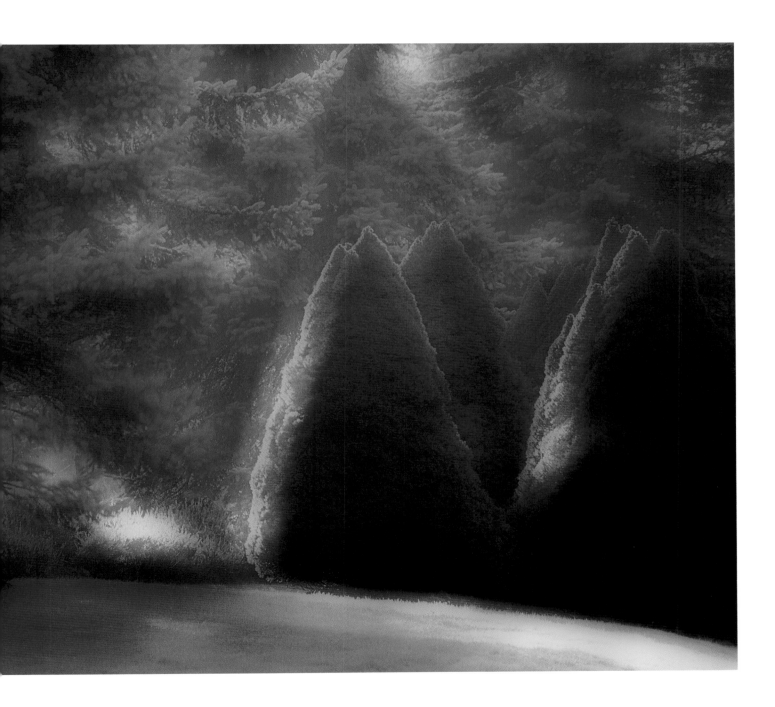

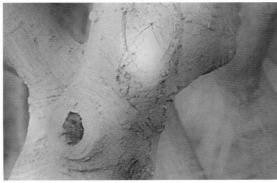

Above and opposite: Tel Aviv, Israel

Above and opposite: wildflowers of Texas

CROSS DREAMSCAPES

A good friend shared her exploration of montages with me. She combines a vertical slide with a horizontal one to produce a square image. Intrigued, I tried this technique, and I loved the effect. I call them "cross dreamscapes," as the paired pieces of film form a cross when placed on top of each other. Unrelated images can work as well as photographs of the same subject matter. I have had success with cross dreamscapes of water surfaces, icebergs, deserts, old cars, plants (especially leaves) and totem poles. The results have an abstract, painterly quality, reminiscent of Kandinsky's colour studies.

As with the other types of dreamscape, if the images are tonally dark they will need to be overexposed. To put a cross dreamscape together, you'll need archival tape. Tape the edge of each slide to the lighter part of a GEPE glassless mount (the piece without the tabs that hold the film) and snap the two mounts together. The slide mounts mask off part of the film, creating a square image. I scan the dreamscape, saving it to disk, and have a duplicate slide made by a good professional lab. I then take the original montage apart, as I don't want any moisture to collect between the pieces of film, making them stick together.

Opposite: Kingston Creek, New Brunswick

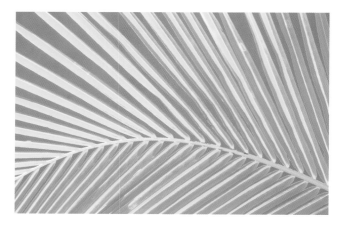

The image on the opposite page is the result of combining the two photographs above. I sometimes look in my existing files for slides I can play with. I thought these fronds had potential, so I looked at the possibilities on my light table, rotating the slides on top of one another. They worked well as mirror dreamscapes, but this cross dreamscape pleased me tremendously. I scanned it and made a few prints. I can now use either or both of the above images for other dreamscapes.

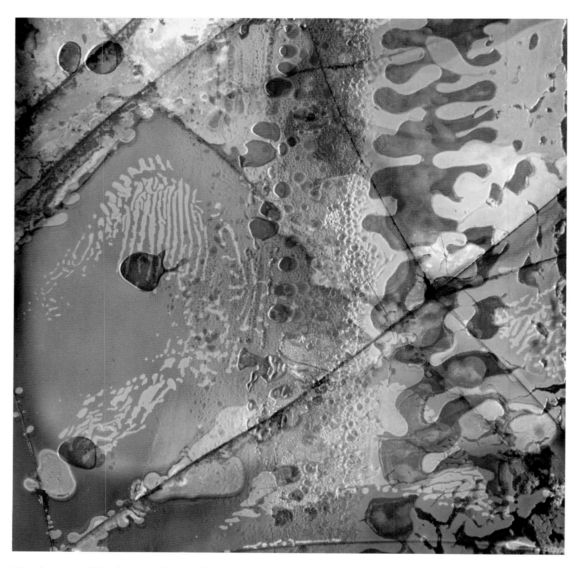

I had many slides from a shoot of an old car graveyard, so I combined images of glass from the cars' windshields. I love the abstractions and the intimacy of the square format.

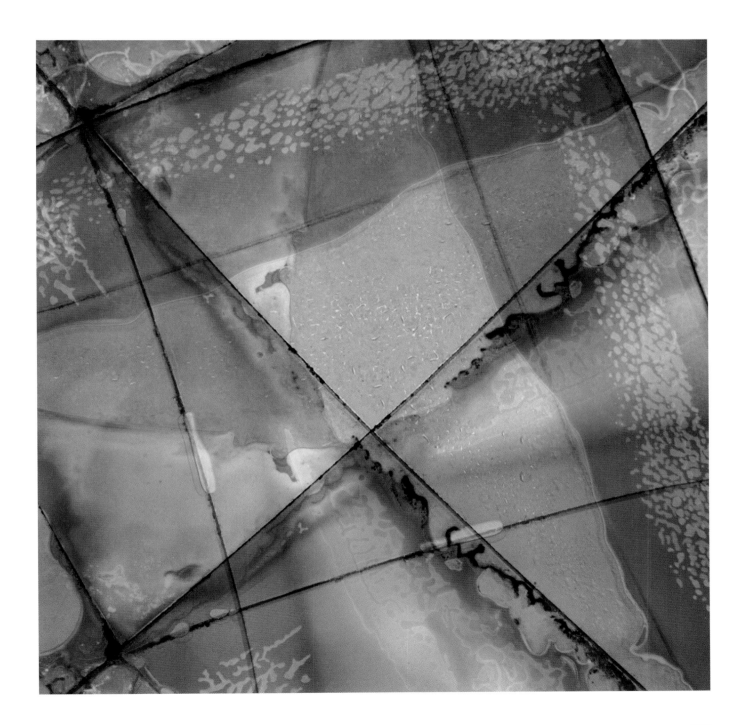

This cross dreamscape was created
with two identical images of cacti.
The symmetry is obvious.

To create the image above, I crossed two different images of peacock feathers. The result is a beautiful asymmetry.

The dreamscape on the opposite page was created by crossing the two identical photos above (see right). The cross of the arches creates an interesting movement that is emphasized by the thrust of the oblique, producing a very geometric photograph.

CONSONANCE

"Moving water ... has a fascinating vitality. It has power and grace and associations. It has a thousand colors and a thousand shapes, yet it follows laws so definite that the tiniest streamlet is an exact replica of a great river."

RODERICK HAIG BROWN

Above: Moving water at sunset, Little River, Saint John, New Brunswick
Opposite: Reflections on water, Aruba

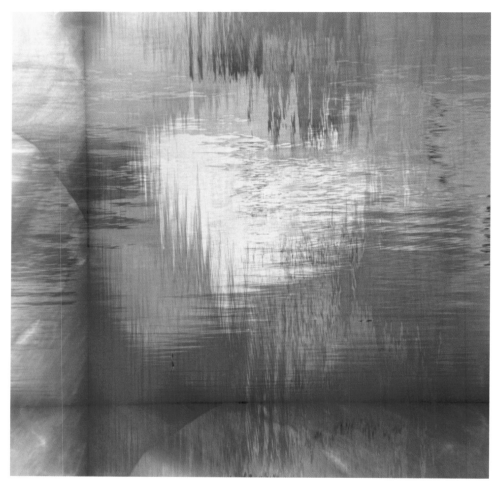

Above and opposite: an iceberg in coastal water, Alaska

Above: Kingston Lake, New Brunswick

Opposite: Saint John River, New Brunswick

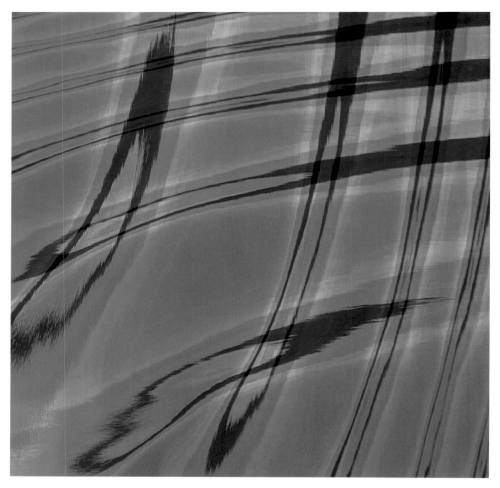

Above and opposite: sailboat wake, Alaska

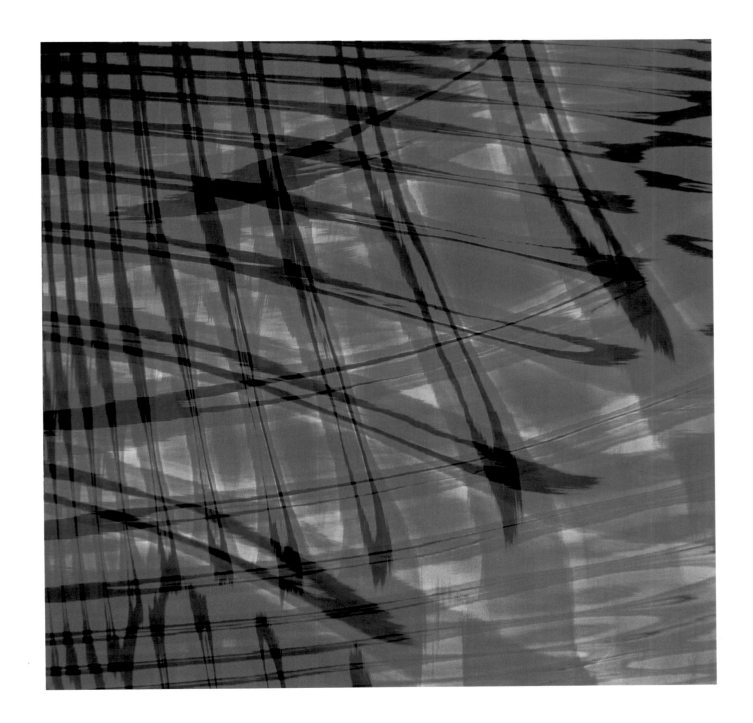

EXOTICA

"The flower is the poetry of reproduction. It is an example of the eternal seductiveness of life."

Jean Giraudoux, *The Enchanted*, 1933

Above: agave plant and anthurium / Opposite: Succulent, South Africa

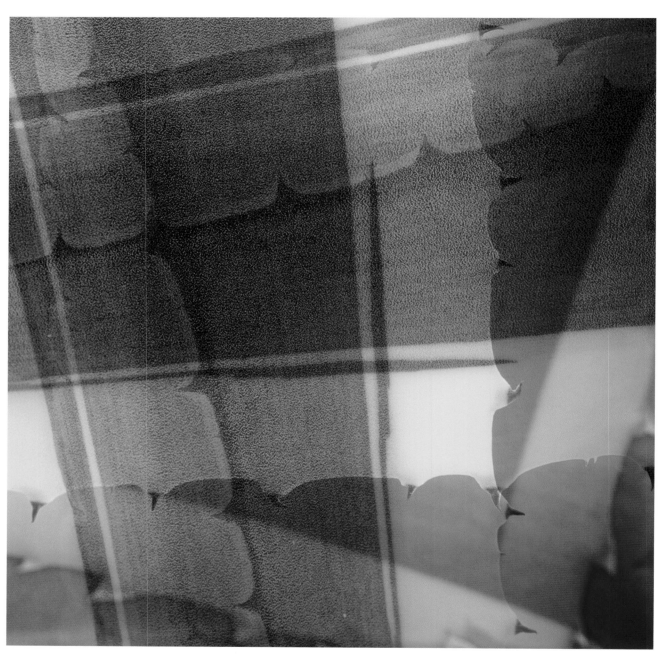

Above and opposite: desert plants, Burlington Botanical Garden, Ontario

Above and opposite : Bird of Paradise with mosaic glass, Burlington Botancial Garden, Ontario

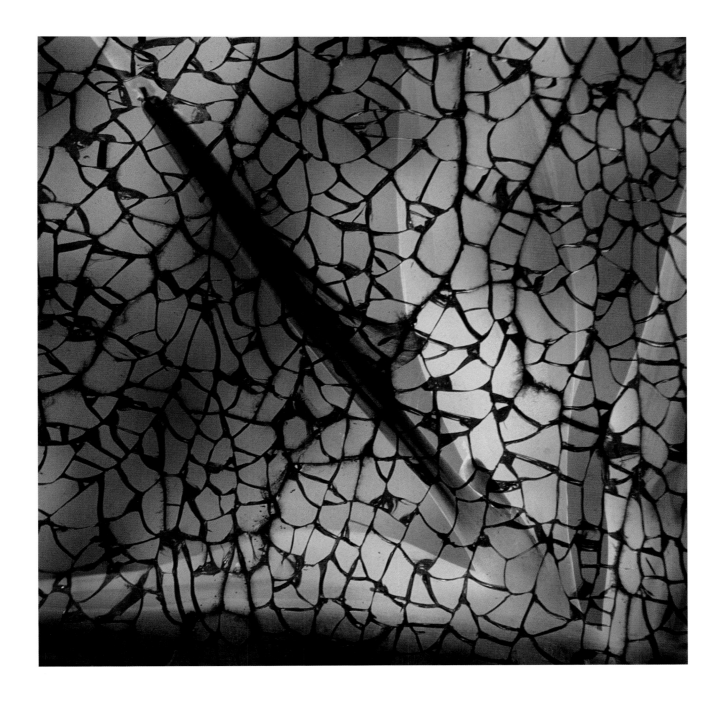

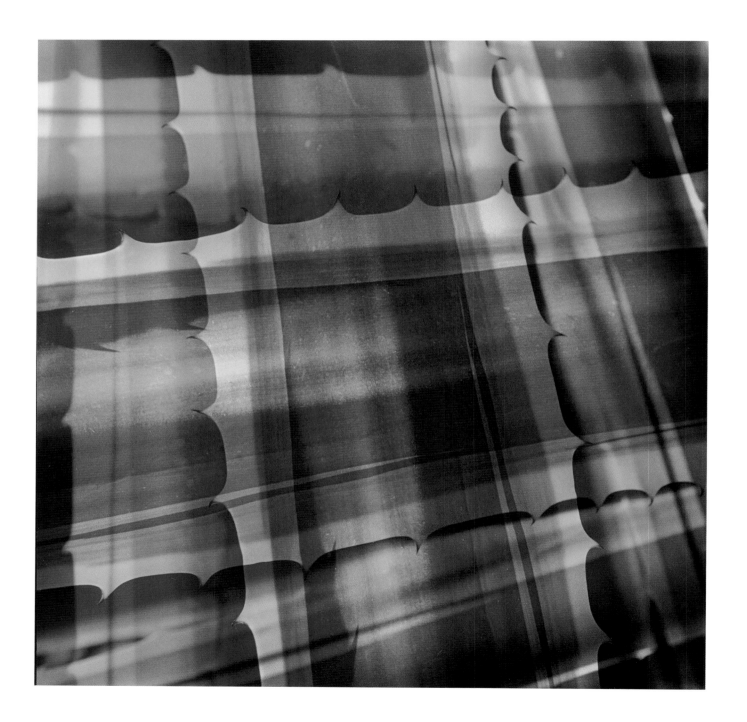

Above and opposite: desert plants,
Burlington Botanical Garden, Ontario

THANK YOU...

Parker, for your continuous support and for making me laugh every day.
You are a true inspiration.

Freeman, for your friendship and generosity, and for paving the way.

Susan Meyer, for your advice and your help. You're a wonderful friend.

Craig York at Image House Digital, for your scanning expertise.

Andrew Smith at PageWave Graphics, for an elegant design.

Sue Sumeraj, for shaping the text.